# Table of Contents

## Wrap-Ups

# Introduction

The purpose of this book is to provide you with a great collection of proven warm-ups and wrap-ups that you can use quickly and effectively to open or close your group or class.

## Warm-Ups

The purpose of a warm-up is to open your group, class, or meeting in a fun way that helps people connect to each other and to the subject of the meeting in an interactive and relationship-building way. All the warm-ups in this book are indexed by topic and Scripture to help you in selecting the warm-up that will work best for your meeting. In general, when planning your meeting, allow fifteen minutes for a warm-up.

## Wrap-Ups

The purpose of a wrap-up is to close your group, class, or meeting in an appropriate and meaningful way. Many of these are fun and light-hearted, while others are more serious. A wrap-up helps to bring home the point of a given meeting or study. The wrap-ups in this course are not intended to take the place of a closing prayer time. Some of the wrap-ups include prayer, but you are encouraged when planning your meeting to schedule time for the wrap-up (generally around fifteen minutes) as well as for closing prayer. Like the warm-ups, the wrap-ups in this book are indexed by topic and Scripture.

## Icons

You will notice that for each warm-up and wrap-up in this book there are icons. Every exercise has a main icon identifying it as either a warm-up or a wrap-up. However, in addition to the warm-up and wrap-up symbols, there are a few additional images. The purpose of these additional icons is to help you identify at a glance the following information:

## Especially for Couples Groups

While most of the warm-ups and wrap-ups in this book can be used in any group setting, when you see the above icon you will know that this exercise is particularly for use in a couples group. Twenty-nine of the 101 exercises in this book carry this designation.

### A Bookend Exercise

When you see this icon, it indicates there is a related exercise, a book-end, which you may want to use as well. For example, if you were to use the warm-up *Commitments* (page 33), you then might want to close your meeting with the wrap-up *Committed* (page 79). Ten of the warm-ups have this symbol, directing you to related wrap-ups.

### Supplies Required

This icon indicates that supplies are required for this particular warm-up or wrap-up. The supplies are generally easy-to-find items. The use of supplies can help bring a more active and visual experience to your class or group. Seventeen of the 101 warm-ups and wrap-ups have this symbol.

### In General

When using these exercises, you are encouraged to see yourself in the role of a facilitator—one who encourages people, helps group members feel more comfortable, keeps things moving forward, and helps the members of your group or class discover things for themselves. You are encouraged to sample the variety of exercises in this book. Be mindful that not all adults learn in the same way. And to help you track the exercises you use, there is a handy checklist in the back of this book that you are encouraged to use.

Most of all, have fun and enjoy! And remember, with the purchase of this book you have permission to photocopy any of the exercises for use in the immediate group or class you are leading.

# Lifestyles of the Stressed and Frazzled

**Topic:** Busyness

**Scripture:** Matthew 6:25-34; Philippians 4:6-7

Do you have a case of hurry sickness? Review the following symptoms, placing a check next to the ones you have.

"STRESS BUILDERS AND BUSTERS," PAGE 86

___ I prefer to be first in line at a red light and will change lanes to be so.

___ I always seem to be running just a little late.

___ I rely on my ability to multitask (for example, drive, talk on my cell phone, drink my coffee, and shave or apply makeup, all at the same time).

___ My desk could be declared a disaster area.

___ When I'm in the express lane at the grocery store, I count the number of items in the basket ahead of me.

___ I find myself rushing even when I have no need to rush.

___ I have a difficult time saying no when people ask me to do things.

___ I have all my important phone numbers on speed dial.

___ I would be lost without my PDA (personal digital assistant) or cell phone by my side.

___ I find myself wishing the microwave would hurry up.

___ I have been known to complain about the service at a fast-food restaurant being too slow.

___ I have to check e-mail at least once a day (including the weekend).

Your score: _____ (Give yourself one point for each symptom checked.)

## Hurry Scale

1 to 3: You have a healthy pace in life.
4 to 6: You have a mild case of hurry sickness.
7 to 9: You have a full-blown case of hurry sickness.
10 to 12: You have a terminal case of hurry sickness.

After everyone has determined his or her score, answer these questions:

- **What was your score?**

- **Which symptom did you identify with the most? Why?**

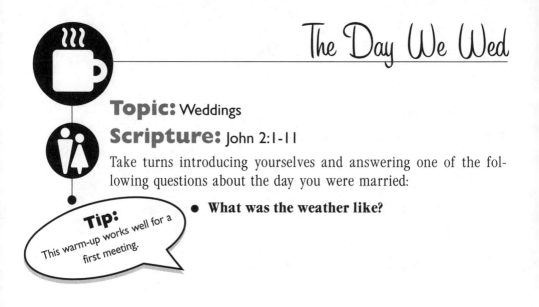

# The Day We Wed

**Topic:** Weddings

**Scripture:** John 2:1-11

Take turns introducing yourselves and answering one of the following questions about the day you were married:

- **What was the weather like?**

**Tip:** This warm-up works well for a first meeting.

- **Who traveled the farthest to attend your wedding?**

- **What special song was sung?**

- **What happened that you didn't expect?**

# Leader or Servant?

**Topics:** Leadership; Servanthood

**Scripture:** Matthew 20:20-28; Mark 10:35-45

In two groups, review the list of personal characteristics that follows. One group should circle five characteristics from the list that its members feel are most important for a leader. The other group should select five characteristics that are most important for a servant.

| | | |
|---|---|---|
| honest | humble | articulate |
| intelligent | compassionate | persuasive |
| diplomatic | innovative | optimistic |
| loving | dependable | loyal |
| risk-taker | extroverted | likeable |
| self-confident | outspoken | goal-oriented |
| flexible | decisive | courageous |
| motivated | patient | forgiving |

After both groups have made their selections, relate which words were picked and discuss the following questions:

- **Why did your group pick the words it did?**

- **Would you classify the two lists as very similar or very different? Why?**

- **How are leading and serving different? similar?**

# The Hurried Family

**Topics:** Busyness

**Scripture:** Psalm 46:10

"Be Still," Page 87

Read aloud the following case study:

From the outside, 911 Cliff Drive looked like the place to be. There were two new cars and a fishing boat in the garage, and a new addition was being added to the back of the house. The back yard had all the amenities: a pool and a hot tub, a nice deck, and a professionally constructed treehouse. Harry and Henrietta Hurried, the occupants at 911 Cliff Drive, were a bright, successful couple with three children (who all, by the way, arrived *before* their due dates).

Harry was an insurance salesman, and he coached their younger son's fourth-grade basketball team. Henrietta worked six hours a day at a local elementary school and co-led their daughter's Girl Scout troop. In addition, she and Harry took their kids to various practices and lessons—gymnastics, piano, and soccer. Their ninth-grade son was involved in band and school sports. Every game and concert was important, so Harry or Henrietta made almost every one of them.

The Hurrieds also were heavily involved in their church. On Sundays they taught Sunday school and attended worship, and on Wednesday evenings they participated in a HomeBuilders group. When the youth group at church needed a high school sponsor, the Hurrieds were asked. Harry wasn't sure they could make the commitment, but couldn't see how they could say no.

Life in the Hurried house started early and ended late. Harry and Henrietta would collapse into bed exhausted. Before falling asleep, they would briefly talk about the next day's schedule. Weekends didn't provide much of a break, as Saturdays were often spent going to ballgames and shopping or trying to get their boat out to the lake, and Sundays were busy with church and trying to get ready for the week ahead.

Harry and Henrietta both sensed something was wrong with their lifestyle. They felt that they really didn't spend much time with their children outside of shuttling them to different activities, and they weren't as close as they once had been. They were starting to drift apart but didn't know what to do.

● In what ways can you relate to the Hurrieds?

● Following are some statements Harry and Henrietta might make to justify their hurried lifestyle:

"I know we should spend more time together as a couple…we'll make up for it in the future."

"I wish we both didn't have to work, but we need the money."

"You can't say no to your church—after all, it's the Lord's work."

"It's important for children to be involved in lots of activities. It's a competitive world, and they need a variety of experiences if they are to get into a good college and be successful."

● How would you evaluate these statements? Pick one statement to respond to. Do you agree? disagree? Explain.

# Getting to Know You

**Topic:** Introductions

**Scripture:** Genesis 2:18-24; 24:61-67

Introduce yourselves as a couple by telling the group one of the following things about your relationship (talk briefly to decide what to share):

- when and where you met

- one fun or unique date before your marriage

- one humorous or romantic time from your honeymoon or early married life

# A Team Sport

**Topic:** Teamwork

**Scripture:** I Corinthians 12:12-26

Take turns introducing yourselves and answering one or two of the following questions:

- **What team, group, or organization do you really admire? Why?**

- **What team do you follow? Why do you support this team?**

- **What has been one of the best teams, clubs, groups, or organizations you have been a part of? Explain what made being a part of that team a good experience.**

# Likely Responses

**Topic:** Attitude

**Scripture:** Ephesians 4:22-24; Philippians 2:1-8

Working individually, select the response that you believe your spouse would most likely have in each of the following situations. Mark that response with an S. Then select the response that you would most likely have, and mark it with an M.

1. **The family dog has just tracked mud across the newly cleaned carpet. Likely first response**

   ___ get really mad at the dog

   ___ laugh

   ___ cry

   ___ launch an immediate and intense investigation into how this happened and who is responsible

   ___ get mad at someone in the family for allowing this to happen

   ___ clean up the mess

2. **Your spouse has just defeated you in a friendly game of tennis. Likely first response**

   ___ congratulate the winner on his or her skill and prowess

   ___ demand a rematch

   ___ suddenly grow unusually quiet and moody

   ___ complain about a sore elbow

   ___ silently vow revenge and patiently wait for just the right opportunity

3. **You've just received a call from your spouse that there's been "a little accident" with the car. Likely first response**

   ___ immediately ask whether he or she is all right

   ___ immediately ask whether the car is all right

   ___ immediately ask whose fault the accident was

   ___ immediately think about the impact to the insurance rate

After marking your responses, get with your spouse and compare results. Then discuss these questions as a group:

- **How well did you predict your spouse's responses?**

- **When you find yourself in a situation like one of the previous scenarios, how much does your anticipation of your spouse's response affect you?**

- **What effect can the "right" response from your spouse have on you?**

# A Match Made in Paradise

**Topic:** Marriage

**Scripture:** Genesis 2:18-24

In separate groups of men and women, come up with lists of things you think made Adam and Eve's marriage good. For example, "They didn't have to face the dilemma of whose family to visit during the next holiday." Have fun with this activity.

After a few minutes, come back together, share your lists, and answer the following questions:

- **In what ways are the lists similar?**

- **How are they different?**

- **What discoveries did you make in your discussion?**

# Please Pass the Roles

**Topics:** Chores; Roles

**Scripture:** Ephesians 5:21-33

Read the following list of household chores, and assign an M to each task you regularly perform, an S to each chore your spouse usually does, and a B to the tasks that you share. If a task is listed that doesn't apply, place the letter X next to it.

___ take out the trash
___ make the bed
___ prepare dinner
___ clean out the garage
___ hang wallpaper
___ maintain the vehicle(s)
___ wash dishes
___ dust
___ clear the table
___ run errands (such as to the bank, post office, and cleaners)

___ do the laundry
___ mow the lawn
___ clean the bathroom
___ pay the bills
___ shop for groceries
___ vacuum
___ paint the house (interior)
___ paint the house (exterior)
___ make general household repairs
___ drive (when you're in the car together)

"JOB DESCRIPTIONS," PAGE 85

After everyone has finished assigning the appropriate letters, answer the following questions:

● **What was the total number of tasks to which you assigned the letter M? the letter B?**

● **Within this group what, if any, chores were exclusively done by men or women? Why do you think this is? How do you feel about that?**

● **What, if any, insight about marriage does this exercise demonstrate to you?**

*Best Friends*

**Topic:** Friendship

**Scripture:** Proverbs 17:17; 18:24; John 15:12-15

Share with the group your answer to one of the following questions:

- **Who was your best friend when you were growing up, and what made you close?**

- **Think about someone who helped you make the transition to a new school, job, neighborhood, or church. What did that person do that helped you the most?**

- **What's the closest group of friends that you've been a part of?**

# Dream House

**Topics:** Dream house; Marriage

**Scripture:** Psalm 127:1; Matthew 7:24-27

Tear a blank sheet of paper in half. Individually, take two or three minutes to draw out a one-floor plan of what you would consider your dream house—the home you would love to build if you could. After you've finished, get with your spouse to compare floor plans and answer the following questions:

- **In what ways are your floor plans similar?**

- **What are the biggest differences?**

**Supplies:**
For this warm-up, each couple will need one sheet of paper and pens or pencils.

- **How would you compare this exercise with marriage?**

When each couple has had time to answer these questions, report to the group on your comparisons of this exercise with marriage.

# 168-Hour Week

"168-
HOUR
WEEK"
(PART 2),
PAGE 113

**Topics:** Priorities; Time

**Scripture:** Ecclesiastes 3:1-8; Ephesians 5:15-17

We all have 168 hours to spend each week. Recap your last week by filling out the following weekly time sheet. For each category, enter your best estimate of how much time you spent during the last week.

___ work (your primary job—include getting ready and commuting time)

___ sleep (include getting ready for bed)

___ exercise

___ other work (things like household chores)

___ TV or computer (personal Web surfing, e-mail)

___ marriage (time spent with your spouse)

___ family/friends (time spent with kids, extended family, and friends)

___ God (include Bible study, prayer, and time at church)

___ errands/shopping

___ meals (include preparation time)

___ other: _____

**Total: 168 hours**

After you've completed your time sheet, discuss the following:

- **What did you spend too much time doing? too little time doing?**

# Down Memory Lane

**Topic:** Memories

**Scripture:** Proverbs 10:7; Philippians 3:12-14

Share a childhood memory recalled by one of these questions:

- **What positive experience—a particular accomplishment, for example, or something someone said about you—can still make you feel good to this day?**

- **What not-so-positive experience—perhaps an embarrassing moment—can you laugh about today, although the memory still makes you cringe?**

After everyone has had a chance to share, take turns answering this question:

- **In general when you think back to your childhood, how do you feel?**

  ☐ I get butterflies in my stomach, and my palms get sweaty.

  ☐ I'm glad it's over.

  ☐ I wish I could do it all again.

  ☐ It makes me smile.

  ☐ Other: _____.

# Guess Who

**Topic:** Self-descriptions

**Scripture:** Psalm 139:13-16

On a piece of paper or an index card, list three or four words or phrases that describe you, and then give your list to the leader. To make this more interesting, use descriptions that may not be obvious immediately. For example, don't describe yourself by height and hair color. Instead think about traits (such as patience), talents (like tennis), or tendencies (maybe shyness).

When all the lists have been turned in, the leader will, in random order, read the lists to the group. After each description, write your guess about who in the group the list describes. After all the lists have been read, share your guesses, and then answer the following questions:

**Supplies:** For this warm-up, everyone will need an index card or a piece of paper and a pen or pencil.

- **In what way do words have the power to paint pictures in our minds?**

- **What is one way you are a different person today than you were five or ten years ago?**

# A Piece of the Pie

## Topics: Priorities; Schedules
## Scripture: Ephesians 5:15-17

Use the diagram that follows to make a pie chart of your typical day.
Assign times to your diagram for the applicable activities below:

"ANOTHER
PIECE OF
THE PIE,"
PAGE 70

- sleeping
- eating (including preparation time)
- driving
- working
- television
- Bible study/prayer
- other: _____

- chores (such as paying bills, doing laundry, taking out the trash, and running errands)
- time with your spouse
- time with children
- exercise
- Internet

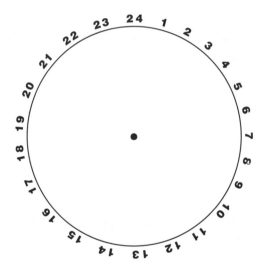

After charting your typical day, answer these questions:

- **What priorities does your schedule reflect?**

- **Which areas in your life generally lose out to other things?**

*Practiced Prayer*

**Topic:** Prayer

**Scripture:** Matthew 6:5-13; Luke 11:1-4

Whether or not you grew up in a Christian home, you learned about prayer as you observed the attitudes and practices of family, friends, church members, or even characters in television shows and movies.

- **For fun, recite aloud any memorized prayers you still remember.**

- **What do you remember about your concept of prayer as a child?**

- **How has your concept of prayer changed since you were a child? Why?**

# I Love to Tell the Story

**Topic:** Bible

**Scripture:** 2 Timothy 3:16; Hebrews 4:12

Begin by sharing one or two of the following with the group:

- **a favorite Bible story from your childhood and why it's a favorite**

- **a Bible passage that has been particularly meaningful in your life**

- **the influence the Bible has had on your life and why**

*Popcorn*

## Topics: Communication; Listening

## Scripture: Proverbs 15:1; James 1:19-20

"BRIAN AND LINDA REVISITED," PAGE 83

Read aloud the following case study, choosing a reader for each of the three parts (narrator, Linda, and Brian). After reading the case study, discuss the accompanying questions.

**Narrator:** It has been a long, trying Monday for both Brian and his wife, Linda. Fall is Brian's favorite time of year because of his love for professional football, and Monday night is his favorite night of the week. Linda enjoys an occasional game as well and has joined him in the family room. The end of the day and the smell of hot popcorn promise a pleasant evening at home together—or do they?

**Linda:** I wonder why our new neighbors always leave their garage door open. Wouldn't you think they would be afraid of someone stealing their things?

**Brian:** I don't know.

**Linda:** I think we need to have them over sometime. I wonder if they know anyone around here. Maybe next weekend we could invite them and some of our friends over for a barbecue.

**Brian:** Uh huh.

**Linda:** I can tell you are really concerned about these people, Brian.

**Brian:** Hmmmm.

**Linda:** Your mom called yesterday, honey. She says that all your dad wants for his birthday this year is another TV set—for the bathroom. Can you imagine, a TV set in the bathroom?

**Brian:** What kind does he want?

**Linda:** Are you just like your dad? If you had a TV in the bathroom you'd never come out—and you're in there too long as it is.

**Brian:** Would you mind getting some salt for the popcorn?

**Linda:** *(A little heated)* You get your own salt!

**Brian:** Now wait a minute! You know I don't want to miss any of this game. Now get the salt!

WARM-UPS

**Linda:** *(Sarcastically)* I think it would be all right for you to miss just a little of the game. You certainly have missed a lot of this conversation.

**Brian:** *(With strong emotion)* Look, I'm not in this room to talk. Do I have to take this TV set into the bathroom to watch this game? Maybe I will go in there—at least I won't be interrupted!

**Linda:** *(Sarcastically)* Fine! Shall I slip the salt under the door, or do you want to come out during a commercial?

- **What poor listening habits are Brian and Linda exhibiting?**

- **How do poor listening habits create conflict?**

Put yourself in Brian and Linda's place:

- **If you were Brian, how could you better listen to Linda?**

- **If you were Linda, what could you have done to get Brian to listen better?**

# Invisible Power

**Topics:** Direction; Holy Spirit

**Scripture:** Ezekiel 36:27; Matthew 6:33; John 16:13; Romans 8:9-14

Line up side by side, with everyone holding an uninflated balloon and facing in the same direction. When your leader gives the signal, throw your balloon as far out in front of you as you can.

Retrieve your balloon and inflate it. Don't tie it off, but hold the opening closed so that the air doesn't escape. Again line up with the other group members, aim your balloon out in front of you, and at your leader's signal let it go. After the confusion and laughter, pick up your balloon, and sit down to discuss the following questions:

**Supplies:**
For this exercise, everyone will need one uninflated balloon.

- **Which time did the balloon travel a greater overall distance?**

- **What made the difference in the way the balloon traveled?**

- **How might this activity be like God working in a person's life through the power of the Holy Spirit?**

# Reflections

**Topic:** Following Christ

**Scripture:** Matthew 4:18-22; Ephesians 5:1-2

Stand facing a partner. For the start of this activity, the person standing closest to the leader will be a "reflectee," and the other person will be a "reflector." Reflectees will make any motions or facial expressions they want to, and reflectors will move as if they were mirror reflections. After about thirty seconds, switch roles. After another thirty seconds, sit down to discuss the following questions with the whole group:

- **What was it like to try to follow your partner's actions?**

- **What was most important to successful following?**

- **How is this like trying to follow Jesus?**

**Topic:** Conflict

**Scripture:** Hebrews 12:14-15; 1 Peter 3:8-12

Conflict is inevitable when two people live together. A number of seemingly small things can often spark arguments and conflict. Tell the group about one of these that has caused a now-humorous conflict in your marriage. Or tell about one not in this list that stands out in your mind. Conflict may occur concerning

- which lights to keep on,
- sleeping with a window open or closed,
- where to set the thermostat,
- what radio station to listen to (and at what volume),
- where clothing is put after it's taken off,
- the proper way to hang toilet paper (over or under),
- whether or not to set the alarm (and for what time),
- whether the cap is kept on the toothpaste tube,
- who makes the bed and how,
- who locks the doors and turns out the lights at bedtime, and
- how long a turn signal should be on.

# Commitments

**Topics:** Focus; Priorities

**Scripture:** Matthew 6:28-34; Philippians 4:8-9; Hebrews 12:1-2

"COMMITTED," PAGE 79

Think back to when you were a teenager—specifically, your high school years. During high school, to what were you most committed? From the list that follows, rank the top three things you were most committed to as a teenager in high school.

| | |
|---|---|
| __ music | __ God |
| __ schoolwork | __ cars |
| __ boyfriend/girlfriend | __ work |
| __ sports | __ church/youth group |
| __ a club or organization | __ family |
| __ friends | __ other: _____ |

After everyone has had a chance to tell what he or she was committed to, discuss the following:

- **What effect—positive or negative—did this commitment have on your life?**

- **How was the top item you listed reflected in your schedule?**

**Topic:** Trials

**Scripture:** Psalm 55:22; 2 Corinthians 4:16-18; James 1:1-2

Discuss the following question for each of the events that follow:

What are typical struggles or trials a couple faces when

- they're newly married?
- they've had their first baby?
- they try to figure out and live by a budget?
- they move a thousand miles from "home"?
- they have a teenager in the house?
- old age sets in?

# Who Would You Trust?

**Topic:** Trust

**Scripture:** Psalm 118:8-9; Proverbs 29:25;
Matthew 10:11-16

"TRUST
BUSTERS
AND
BUILDERS,"
PAGE 81

Select two or three of these questions to respond to.

Who would you trust

- with your car?

- to tell you if your breath was bad?

- to pray for you?

- to give you directions to someplace you haven't been before?

- for an objective opinion on whether your outfit goes together?

- for advice on the stock market?

- for marriage advice?

- for a movie recommendation?

After everyone has shared his or her selections, discuss the following:

- **What qualities make someone trustworthy?**

# By the Numbers

**Topic:** Introductions

**Scripture:** Psalm 77:11-12

As a fun way of better getting to know everyone in the group, work together to calculate the grand total within this group for each of the following items:

- number of years married

- number of kids living at home

- number of household moves since marrying

- current number of pets

- approximate number of miles from home to this group's meeting place

**Tip:**
This is a good warm-up for a first meeting.

# May I Borrow Your Car?

**Topic:** Lending

**Scripture:** Galatians 6:9-10

You have loaned your brand-new car to your friend Bill. When Bill returns the car, it has a crumpled fender, a broken headlight, and a missing bumper. When Bill hands you the keys, he apologizes for the damage and asks whether you would mind loaning him the car again next week.

- **What would you say to Bill?**

- **Why do we expect our friends to treat our property differently than Bill did?**

- **When has something like this happened to you?**

- **How is this situation similar to how we sometimes care for what God gives us?**

# Thank You, Aunt Harriet!

**Topics:** Inheritance; Stewardship

**Scripture:** Matthew 25:14-30; Luke 12:13-21; 19:11-27

You have just been notified that your great-aunt Harriet passed away at the age of one hundred. Her will designates fifty thousand dollars in cash for you. There's only one condition: It all must be spent within thirty days.

Individually, make a list of how you would use the money.

| Item | Estimated Cost |
|------|----------------|
|      |                |

**For Extra Impact:** To add an element of fun to this exercise, consider handing out play money to everyone to represent his or her inheritance.

**Total: $50,000**

After everyone has given an account of his or her funds, discuss these questions:

- **What did you consider as you decided how to use the money?**

- **Think of an item that you initially thought about adding to your list but ultimately decided against. Why did you decide against that item?**

# Bad Hair Day?

**Topic:** Your day

**Scripture:** Psalm 118:24

Take a few minutes to tell one another about the kind of day you've had by answering these questions:

- **What word or words from the following list would best describe the kind of day you've had today?**

  - typical
  - fantastic
  - pleasant
  - terrible
  - exhausting
  - trying

  - exhilarating
  - encouraging
  - forgettable
  - blessed
  - poor
  - other: _____

- **What one thing would you say most contributed to the kind of day you've had?**

- **What could make this a better day for you?**

# The Way We Were

**Topics:** Contentment; Finances

**Scripture:** Proverbs 23:4-5; Philippians 4:10-13;
I Timothy 6:6-10; Hebrews 13:5

Take a few minutes to reminisce by answering these questions:

- **What was your biggest financial need when you were first married?**

- **How has your financial situation changed since you were first married? In what ways is it the same?**

- **What do you think is the best purchase you've made as a couple? the worst or most disappointing?**

- **What one lesson about money have you learned that has really stuck with you?**

# What I Like, How About You?

**Topic:** Preferences

**Scripture:** Galatians 3:26-29

In each of the following six categories, how do you see yourself? How do you see your spouse? How does your spouse see you? On the spectrum lines for each category, place a Y where you see yourself and an S where you see your spouse. When you've finished, compare your results with your spouse's! Then share with the group the one category in which your ratings most closely agreed or disagreed.

## MUSIC

A little bit country                    A little bit rock 'n' roll

## MOVIES

Comedy                                             Drama

## NUTRITION

Health food                                    Junk food

## FINANCES

"You can't take it with you."      "A penny saved is a penny earned."

## VACATION

Go, go, go.                                      Just relax.

## TECHNOLOGY

Online                                             Offline

# As Advertised

**Topics:** Covetousness; Possessions; Wants

**Scripture:** Matthew 6:19-24; Mark 10:17-23;
Luke 12:13-21

Think about some memorable advertisements you've seen or heard recently.

- **Which ad or commercial has been**

  the most appealing to you?

  the worst or most obnoxious?

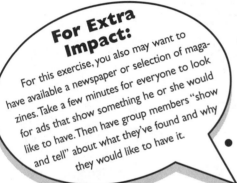

**For Extra Impact:**
For this exercise, you also may want to have available a newspaper or selection of magazines. Take a few minutes for everyone to look for ads that show something he or she would like to have. Then have group members "show and tell" about what they've found and why they would like to have it.

  the most outrageous?

  normal?

- **What does our culture communicate about money and possessions through advertisements?**

# Vive la Différence!

**Topics:** Differences; Similarities

**Scripture:** Ecclesiastes 4:9-12; Romans 12:3-8

For each of the following categories, decide whether you and your spouse are more similar or different. Individually take a minute to complete the following exercise. For each item, circle either S (representing similar) or D (representing different).

| | | |
|---|---|---|
| Personality | S | D |
| Sense of humor | S | D |
| Musical tastes | S | D |
| Family background | S | D |
| Special interests | S | D |

After completing this exercise, compare results with your spouse, and then answer these questions as a group:

- **Who had the most items marked as similar? different?**

- **What are some ways that differences between a husband and wife might strengthen a marriage?**

- **Discuss together the importance of recognizing differences in dealing with conflict.**

# Giving It Away

**Topic:** Giving

**Scripture:** Matthew 6:19-24; 25:31-40; Acts 20:32-35; 2 Corinthians 9:6-8

If you had one hundred thousand dollars to give away, where would you donate the money? Decide which charitable organizations you would give to and how much you would give to each. Try to come up with at least three organizations you would support.

Organization                           Amount

1.


2.


3.



**Total: $100,000**


After spreading the wealth, report to the group which organizations you gave to and why.

# Something Between Us

**Topics:** Barriers; Communication; Transparency

**Scripture:** Matthew 5:23-24; I Corinthians 1:10;
Ephesians 2:14-18

Form pairs (if married, pair up with your spouse). Each twosome should have an item that represents a communication filter. Turn to your partner, and talk with each other about the kind of day you've had today. However, as you talk, be sure to hold up the filter between you. After everyone has experienced the different filters, discuss the following questions:

- **How did it feel to have the various communication filters between you as you talked?**

**Supplies:**
For this exercise you'll need three different "communication filters": (1) clear—plastic wrap; (2) less clear—tissue paper; and (3) obscured—a piece of paper. Have at least one sample of each for every six people you have in your group.

- **What difference did the type of filter that was between you make in the way that you communicated?**

**Leader:**
Make sure each twosome has one of the three filters, and then start the exercise. As people tell each other about their day, call time after thirty seconds or so, and have the groups trade filters and resume their conversations. Do this a couple of times so that each pair experiences communicating while using each of the three different filters.

- **What are some not-so-visible filters that can affect the transparency between people?**

# To Err Is Human, to Forgive Divine

**Topic:** Forgiveness

**Scripture:** Matthew 18:21-22; Ephesians 4:32;
Colossians 3:13

Choose one or two of the following questions to answer and relate to
the group:

- **When you were a child, who taught you the most about
  what forgiveness is? How did this person teach you?**

- **From your childhood, when do you especially remember
  having to say, "I'm sorry"?**

- **Other than Christ, who do you look to as an example of
  a forgiving person? Why?**

# Insults and Blessings

**Topics:** Blessings; Insults

**Scripture:** 1 Peter 3:8-12

Think about the past week. What insults did you hear others speak? Share one example with the group.

Now think of an uplifting, positive word—a word of blessing. Using this word, write a sentence that affirms your spouse or someone in this group. Then share with that person what you've written.

"PAPER-
THIN
SKIN,"
PAGE 74

After everyone has shared his or her sentences, discuss these questions as a group:

● **Which was easier to think of—an insult or a blessing? Why?**

● **How did it feel to receive a word of blessing?**

**Topic:** Stress

**Scripture:** 2 Corinthians 4:16-18; Galatians 6:2;
1 Peter 5:7

**Tip:** This warm-up works well for a first meeting.

To get to know others in the group, pair up with someone, and use the questions that follow to take turns interviewing each other. (If this is a group of couples, pair up with another couple, with husbands interviewing husbands and wives interviewing wives.)

- **When you hear the word *stress*, what comes to mind?**

- **What is something that caused you stress as a teenager?**

- **What is the most stressful job you've ever had?**

- **How do you like to unwind after a particularly busy or stressful day?**

After everyone has been interviewed, introduce your partner to the group along with one thing you've learned about him or her.

# My Cup Runneth Over

**Topics:** Priorities; Work

**Scripture:** Luke 10:38-42

When everyone has a cup and a rock, form a circle around the pile of household objects. Your goal is to fit as many objects inside your cup (below the rim) as you can, with one condition: You must fit your rock in somewhere. After a few minutes, stop to see who could get the most objects into his or her cup. Then discuss these questions:

- **What is the big thing, or "rock," that takes up most of your time in an ordinary day?**

**Supplies:**

For this warm-up, each person will need a plastic or Styrofoam cup and a rock that will fit in the cup and will take up at least half of the space inside. You'll also need an assortment of household objects that can fit inside the cup—coins, buttons, nails, spools of thread, pieces of cloth, marbles, or whatever is convenient.

- **How would you compare this exercise to the struggle we face in deciding how many other things we can squeeze into a day that is taken up mostly by one thing?**

# Loose Change

**Topic:** Needs

**Scripture:** Luke 12:22-31; Philippians 4:19

Check your pockets or pocketbook for coins. As a group, determine how much money you have collectively in change. Then discuss the following with your spouse:

- **Spending up to but not exceeding the amount of change the group has, what is something you could do for a date?**

Share your idea with the group.

After each couple has had the opportunity to share its idea for a "cheap date," everyone should select one coin at random and answer this question:

- **Look at the date on your coin. What financial need can you remember having in that year?**

# Strings Attached

**Topics:** Relationships; Unity

**Scripture:** Psalm 133:1; Romans 12:9-13; Hebrews 10:24-25

When everyone has five pieces of string, form groups of up to six people. Each group should stand in a circle, with a diameter of about six feet. The challenge of this exercise is for you to quickly become connected to everyone in your circle. When your leader says "Go!" everyone should attempt simultaneously to connect with everyone else in the circle as quickly as possible by running a separate length of string between you and each person in your circle. It doesn't matter whether the strings get tangled, as long as everyone is connected. After everyone is connected, discuss these questions:

**Supplies:**
For this warm-up, each person will need up to five lengths of string, twine, or yarn, approximately six feet long.

- **What difficulties did you face in trying to connect with the others in your circle?**

- **If one person were to fall down or try to walk away while still holding all of his or her strings, what effect would it have on your connection? on your group's connection?**

- **How is this exercise like trying to stay connected to the important people in your life?**

# Hard Times

**Topic:** Hardships

**Scripture:** 2 Corinthians 1:3-7

Choose one of the following questions to answer and share with the group:

- **How many broken bones have you had?**

- **Who is better in a crisis, you or your spouse? Why?**

- **What was the first big crisis (serious or funny) you faced in your marriage?**

- **How has going through a trying time helped you be able to encourage someone else?**

# Your Spiritual Heritage

**Topics:** Church; Evangelism; Family; Spiritual heritage

**Scripture:** Proverbs 22:6; Matthew 28:19-20;
2 Timothy 1:3-7

Whether or not your parents were religious, you learned something about God from them. Begin this session by talking about your spiritual upbringing.

- **What was the spiritual environment in the home in which you grew up?**

- **What kind of spiritual influence have your parents had on you?**

- **What is one of your earliest memories of church?**

- **Based on your spiritual background, how equipped do you feel to tell others about God?**

**Topics:** Following; Leading

**Scripture:** John 13:1-17; I Corinthians 1:10-17

For this warm-up, everyone in the group will have the opportunity to take a brief turn at being the leader. As the leader, you will have unmitigated power to lead however you would like, but there's a catch: Your "reign" lasts only thirty seconds. Before getting underway, take a few minutes to think about what you want to do when it's your turn to be the leader. For example, you may want to lead the group in

- reciting the Lord's prayer
- saying the pledge of allegiance
- singing a song
- repeating a verse you've memorized
- mimicking or repeating an action you do

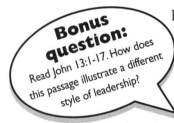

**Bonus question:** Read John 13:1-17. How does this passage illustrate a different style of leadership?

Remember, you have only thirty seconds. If you aren't comfortable being the leader, you can "pass" to the next person. The goal of the group is to follow the leader as closely as possible.

After everyone has had the opportunity to lead, discuss these questions:

- **What was the most important element of being a successful leader in this activity? a successful follower?**

- **Which was harder, to lead or to follow? Why?**

- **How is this exercise like trying to lead others to walk with God? How is it different?**

# Listen Up!

**Topics:** Patience; Understanding

**Scripture:** Proverbs 11:12; 14:29; 1 Corinthians 13:4-7

Read aloud the following case study, choosing a reader for each of the three parts (narrator, Rod, and Cindy). Then discuss the question that follows.

"LISTEN UP!" (EPILOGUE), PAGE 90

> **Narrator:** When Rod arrived home from work, he could tell that his wife, Cindy, was discouraged.
>
> **Rod:** *(Concerned)* Hi, honey. Rough day?
>
> **Cindy:** *(Tired and a little emotional)* Yeah, nothing went right today.
>
> **Narrator:** After dinner and helping the kids with their homework, Rod and Cindy sat down to talk.
>
> **Rod:** So, tell me about your day. What can I do to help?
>
> **Cindy:** *(Frustrated)* I feel like a taxi driver, shuffling children all over town. And what's worse, I don't get paid. Nobody even says thank you! Just today I had to make two extra trips to Shane's school and one to Annie's. First Shane forgot his lunch, and then he called because he didn't have his basketball shoes. That made me late to my women's Bible study, and right in the middle of the fellowship time, I remembered I'd promised Annie that I'd drop a check by the school office for gymnastics. It's like everyone expects good old mom to pick up all the loose ends.
>
> **Narrator:** Rod starts to speak, but Cindy continues.
>
> **Cindy:** And that wasn't even the worst of it. *Your* parents called today and said they want us to come for Thanksgiving. I told them we wouldn't be able to this year. Naturally, they weren't happy. I'm getting tired of the way they try to make us feel guilty every time we don't do what they want. When I suggested that they come here for Thanksgiving, they said, "But we've always done it here—it just wouldn't be the same." Rod, *you* have to talk to them!
>
> **Rod:** *(In a matter-of-fact tone)* Well, first of all, you shouldn't feel obligated to pick up the loose ends for Shane. I really

think you may be mothering him too much. He's fourteen, and it's OK for him to face the consequences of his forgetfulness. I'll talk to him about being more responsible.

And I really think you should take a few minutes before bed to plan the next day. I spend the first twenty minutes at work planning my day, and it really helps. I think I have an extra day planner at the office. I'll bring one home for you. And feel free to call me. Even though my day is usually pretty full, I can break away at times to run something to the kids.

As for my parents, you know it's better for me to bring up the holidays with them. You should have waited to tell them about Thanksgiving. And I know you always feel like we let them get their way, but what are we supposed to do?

**Cindy:** *(Rising and walking away)* Well, you just have an answer for everything!

● **How do you think Rod should have acted with Cindy?**

# Won't You Be My Neighbor?

**Topics:** Love; Neighbors

**Scripture:** Luke 10:25-37

Choose two or three of the following questions to answer and share with the group:

- **As a child, how well did you get along with your siblings? What did you tend to fight or argue about? How did your mom and dad deal with sibling rivalry?**

- **Thinking back to your childhood, who do you remember being your best neighbors? What makes them stand out?**

- **What's the nicest thing a neighbor has ever done for you?**

- **When you were growing up, who in your neighborhood or at school did you have trouble getting along with? Explain.**

- **When do you recall your family helping a stranger in need?**

# Who Are You?

**Topic:** Acceptance

**Scripture:** 1 Samuel 16:7; Romans 15:7; 2 Corinthians 5:16-21; James 2:1-9

To start, have everyone draw a slip of paper that describes a new fictional identity. Read your description to yourself, and take a minute to think about your new identity. Ask yourself: How comfortable would this person be in this group? Then take turns going around the group and introducing yourselves. After everyone has been introduced, discuss the following questions:

**Supplies:**
For this warm-up, make a copy of the descriptions on page 59, and cut them into strips for your group. If you have more than ten people in your group, make extra copies and break into multiple groups.

- **How did you feel about being the person you were?**

- **How accepting did you feel of the others in the group?**

- **What does this exercise illustrate to you about acceptance?**

You are a serious motorcycle enthusiast. You have long hair and lots of tattoos. You recently became a Christian and are interested in learning what being a Christian is all about.

---

You are from a different country. "Home" for you is halfway around the world. You are in this country as a student. You do not speak the language well, and you are having a difficult time adjusting to the culture.

---

Until yesterday you struggled financially, working two jobs just to make ends meet. Today everything is different. You just found out that you've inherited a large sum of money from a distant relative.

---

You are a "spiritual" person. You believe in God—and you believe in just about everything else as well. You are here to see what this Christian group is all about.

---

Your employer has just transferred you to this city. You expect your stuff to arrive this weekend, and you're trying to make friends quickly so you can ask for help unloading your things.

---

You are homeless. Recently your world was turned upside down; you literally lost everything. You're not really sure why you're here. You heard these people were nice and there would be food, so you came.

---

You are extremely skeptical of Christianity. You believe there is a God, but you don't have much use for so-called organized religion. In fact, the only reason you're here is as a favor to your spouse.

---

Congratulations! Your church has just appointed you to be the volunteer in charge of ministry to couples. You've come to the meeting to see how this group is going.

---

You have just experienced the loss of a loved one who died after an extended battle with AIDS. You're trying to deal with your grief and have come to this group looking for support.

---

You are a middle-aged, middle manager at a large company—at least, you were. You've received notice that the company, for which you have worked since graduation, is letting you go. You're not sure what you're going to do next.

---

**Topic:** Your day

**Scripture:** Hebrews 13:3

Take a few minutes to talk about your day by answering these questions:

- **What was the best thing that happened to you today?**

- **What was the worst thing that happened?**

- **What was the funniest thing that happened?**

# Daydreams

**Topics:** Dreams; Hope

**Scripture:** Matthew 7:7-11; John 15:7;
Romans 8:28; 15:4

Share the following with one another:

- **What was the one thing you remember most wanting to do or be when you grew up?**

- **As you grew up, what either encouraged you or discouraged you from achieving your dreams?**

- **What is one dream you have now—no matter how far-fetched—that you think you would like to do or try someday?**

# Neither a Borrower nor Lender Be?

**Topic:** Neighbors

**Scripture:** Luke 6:27-36

Consider the following scenario:

Your neighbors the Wilsons (whom you have been trying to get to go to church with you) borrow items from you on a regular basis. Through the years, they've borrowed tools, camping gear, the occasional missing ingredient for a recipe, and once they even borrowed toilet paper! The problem is they hold onto your things for months, or simply don't return them at all. You've addressed this issue with them in a kind way, but after a weak apology and the return of a few things, they quickly returned to their old ways. You have reached the point at which you have had enough. And now the Wilsons are at your door wanting to borrow your ladder.

- **What would your response to the Wilsons likely be?**

- **What would they need to do to regain your trust? Why?**

# House of Cards

**Topic:** Cooperation

**Scripture:** Proverbs 27:17

Working separately, spend two minutes trying to build a house of cards. Build the tallest structure you can. At the end of two minutes, compare structures. Then, starting from scratch, spend another two minutes trying to build the tallest card structure you can. But this time, work together in groups of two or three. After time expires, discuss these questions:

- **Which structure was taller—the house you built alone or the house you built together?**

**Supplies:**
For this warm-up, you'll need a large stack of cards, such as business cards, playing cards, or index cards.

- **What advantage was there in working together?**

# That Makes Me Mad!

**Topic:** Anger

**Scripture:** I Corinthians 13:4-7; Ephesians 4:26-27; James 1:19-21

## What makes you mad when

- you go grocery shopping (for example, searching for a parking space)?

- you are driving?

- you are trying to get your children to bed at night?

- you are under pressure to finish a project or meet a deadline at work?

After sharing your responses, discuss the following:

- **In the situations you've discussed, what are examples of circumstances that are beyond your control?**

- **Despite the things you can't control in the previous situations, what *can* you control?**

# The In-Laws

**Topic:** Parents

**Scripture:** Ephesians 6:1-4

Read aloud the following case study, choosing a reader for each of the three parts (narrator, Craig, and Karen). After reading the case study, discuss the accompanying questions.

**Narrator:** After several years of apartment living, Craig and Karen bought their first home. And it happened just in time—their second child was due only two months after the closing date. Their purchase was a beautiful, four-bedroom home in a new subdivision. The price had been a little beyond their means, but both Craig's and Karen's parents had given them some money to use toward the down payment.

Craig was happy with their new home until he received some startling news after they moved in. Karen's parents, who lived in the same town, had decided to sell the home they had owned for twenty-five years and were going to move to a house across the street! Karen seemed thrilled. Craig was not. He thought Karen's mother had a controlling personality, but Karen had a difficult time understanding his concern.

**Karen:** They were lonely in that old house. Now we can see them more often, and Mom can help with the kids.

**Craig:** But you see them almost every day anyway! You know how much I like your parents, but we've got to have a life of our own. With them here it will be like they're still in charge of our lives. Your mom will be over here telling us how to raise our kids.

**Karen:** Mom does nothing but help us week after week. Why, just last weekend you didn't have any problem with her baby-sitting our son while we went on a date.

**Craig:** Yes, and I also had to listen to her for fifteen minutes telling me all the things I was doing wrong with Tommy. You'd think she never made any mistakes when she was our age.

**Karen:** She's a parent, Craig. Parents can't stop giving advice just because we've left home. We'll be doing the same thing when we're older. Besides, I don't see you speaking up when your own father puts pressure on you to spend Christmas with them every year.

**Craig:** That's totally different.

**Karen:** No, it's not. You say we need to live our own lives. Have you told your parents that? Have you stood up to them when they try to manipulate us and make us feel guilty just because we want to start our own traditions for the holidays?

**Craig:** You know how hard it is to stand up to my dad.

**Karen:** Yes I do, and that's my point. If we're going to talk about "living our own lives," let's step back and look at everything—not just my parents.

- **What mistakes are the people in this story making?**

- **What do you think Craig and Karen's next step should be?**

- **What happens in a marriage relationship when parents are too clingy or a spouse is still dependent on his or her parents?**

- **How can you be separate from your parents and still honor them?**

# Where Do We Go From Here?

**Topic:** Future

**Scripture:** Jeremiah 29:11-13; Hebrews 10:24-25

As you reach the end of this course, take a few minutes to reflect on your experience. Review the following questions, and write responses to the questions that you can answer. Then relate to the group one or more of your answers.

- **What has this group meant to you during the course of this study? Be specific.**

**Tip:**
This wrap-up is recommended for the last meeting of a course or study.

- **What is the most valuable lesson that you've learned or discovered?**

- **How has this study challenged you?**

- **What would you like to see happen next for this group?**

# Thanks for Your Support!

**Topic:** Affirmation

**Scripture:** I Thessalonians 5:11

Here's an opportunity to recognize some of the people in your life and the contributions they've made to you. Read the descriptions that follow, and write the name of the person who best fits the description. (Don't pick your spouse for more than one item.)

_____ The Rock: solid in times of crisis

_____ Peacemaker: has the gift of defusing conflict

_____ Encourager: brings a smile to your face when you're down

_____ The Sage: full of wise words and good advice

_____ Old Faithful: has been there through thick and thin

_____ Comforter: helps you get through the sad times in life

After making your assignments, share one or two with the group. Then answer these questions:

● **What role do you find yourself playing most often?**

● **What role do you need to play more?**

# A Look at Love

**Topic:** Love

**Scripture:** I Corinthians 13:4-8

Form two groups—men and women—and decide which group will take which column of love descriptions that follow:

**Love**

| | |
|---|---|
| is patient | keeps no record of wrongs |
| is kind | does not delight in evil |
| does not envy | rejoices with truth |
| does not boast | always protects |
| is not proud | always trusts |
| is not rude | always hopes |
| is not self-seeking | always perseveres |
| is not angered | never fails |

In your groups, brainstorm ways you could demonstrate practically, in your marriage, each of the descriptions. Keep the focus on ways *you* could demonstrate these traits, not on what you would like your spouse to do for you. After five to ten minutes, stop so groups can report what they've come up with. Then close with a minute of silent prayer. During this time, reflect on which of the ideas developed in this exercise you will put into practice in your marriage.

"A PIECE
OF THE
PIE,"
PAGE 25

**Topics:** Priorities; Schedules

**Scripture:** Ephesians 5:15-17

At the start of this session, you made a pie chart of your typical day. Now, using the following graph, chart what you would like your typical day to look like.

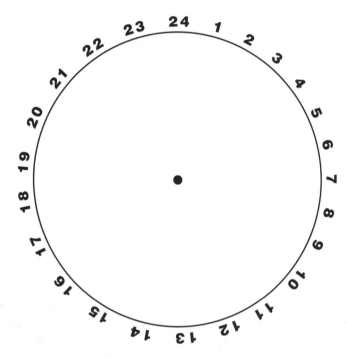

After completing your chart, answer these questions:

- **What is the biggest difference between this chart and the one you made earlier?**

- **What is the biggest obstacle you face in trying to achieve this ideal?**

# It's Puzzling

**Topic:** Bible study

**Scripture:** Joshua 1:8; Psalm 119:11, 105; Acts 17:11

As a group spend some time trying to put together a puzzle without looking at the box top. After you've worked at this for a while, discuss these questions:

- **How is putting together a puzzle without the picture like trying to follow God without studying the Bible?**

**Supplies:**
For this wrap-up, you'll need to have a puzzle—one that is too difficult to put together quickly without looking at a picture of what the puzzle is supposed to look like.

- **Tell about a time you tried to put together something complicated without looking at the instructions. How did it turn out?**

- **What things can you do to ensure that studying the Bible becomes a habit in your life?**

# Serving Each Other

**Topic:** Servanthood

**Scripture:** Galatians 5:13

### Part 1

Individually write as many ways as you can think of in one minute that your spouse has helped you during the past week. When time is up, exchange lists with your spouse. Everyone should then share with the group one thing from the list they've received.

### Part 2

In groups of men and women, brainstorm lists of ways that you can serve your spouse. For example, you might choose to give up your normal Saturday activities and do something with your spouse. After your group has come up with several ideas, select an idea that you'll do this week, and tell your group. (*Don't* tell your spouse what you're planning to do—let it be a surprise!)

# Positive Attributes

**Topic:** Affirmation

**Scripture:** I Thessalonians 4:18

From the following list of positive attributes, pick one that you think someone in this group reflects particularly well. Think about an example that you think illustrates this attribute, and share it with the group.

- honest
- kind
- generous
- courageous
- talented
- forgiving
- patient
- intelligent
- strong
- humble

**Tip:** This wrap-up works best for a group that has been together for a while.

# Paper-Thin Skin

**Topics:** Blessings; Insults

**Scripture:** Psalm 141:3; Ephesians 4:29

Form circles of no more than six people, with each circle having a paper cutout of a person. Pass the paper cutout around the circle. When the cutout comes to you, recall to the group a common negative comment or put-down of some sort, and then tear off a piece of the paper person, and pass the cutout to the next person. After the cutout has been around your group at least once, stop and read Ephesians 4:29.

Now again pass around the paper cutout, but this time share a complimentary or affirming word, and use tape to repair the paper person. After the pieces to your cutout have been reattached, answer the following questions:

"INSULTS AND BLESSINGS," PAGE 47

**Supplies:**
For this wrap-up, you'll need a Bible, tape, and one copy of the paper cutout on the next page for every six people in your group. To be safe, you may want to have at least one copy more than you think you'll need. For a sturdier paper person, make your cutouts from construction paper.

- **How was this experience like what we do to people in real life?**

- **Compare what happened to the paper person with what happens to real people.**

Tip:
For best results, enlarge this page by approximately 150 percent.

**Topic:** Doing God's will

**Scripture:** Micah 6:8; Ephesians 5:1-2

Now it's time to make following God real in your life. Turn to a partner or, if married, to your spouse and talk about specific ways that you can more fully follow God

● at home

● at church

● at work

● in your neighborhood

Commit to doing at least one of these things sometime before your next group meeting. Share with the rest of the group what you plan to do.

# Wishing-Not Well

**Topic:** Devotion

**Scripture:** Romans 12:10; 1 Peter 4:9-10

Each of you should try to come up with five coins. Any coins will do—but you may be giving up these coins permanently. Form a circle if you aren't already in one. Close your eyes, and listen as the leader reads the following questions. Don't answer verbally, but for every question that you must answer yes, toss one coin into the center of the circle. Try not to notice how others around you respond.

- **Within the past month, have you ever let your day get so full that you barely had time to say good morning and good night to your spouse?**

- **Have you recently ignored your spouse—even for a minute—because of something you were watching on television?**

- **Within the past year, have you let work obliterate a time together that the two of you had planned in advance?**

- **Within the past six months, have you let a dispute over children, friends, or activities come between you?**

- **Have you ever let a hobby or other interest consume so much of your time that your spouse felt neglected?**

Now open your eyes, and look at all the coins in the center of your circle. Silently think about how each coin represents at least one dent in someone's marriage relationship. Consider what commitment you may want to make to God about making your marriage more of a priority in your life. If you feel comfortable doing so, share with the group any commitment you want to make. Then gather together all the coins, and have someone buy a treat (however small) for your next meeting.

# Recipe for Relationships

**Topic:** Relationships

**Scripture:** Romans 12:10-18; Colossians 3:12-14

What biblical ingredients make up a good relationship (support your answer with Scripture)?

**Ingredients**

After the group has compiled a list of ingredients, discuss these questions:

- **Recently when has someone close to you seasoned your life with one of these ingredients?**

- **Which of these ingredients could you use most in your life right now? Why?**

# Committed

**Topics:** Focus; Priorities

**Scripture:** Matthew 6:28-34; Philippians 4:8-9; Hebrews 12:1-2

"COMMITMENTS," PAGE 33

To start this session, we looked at what our priorities were earlier in our lives. Now let's look at what our priorities are today. From the list that follows, rank the top three things you currently are most committed to.

___ health/fitness   ___ career

___ education    ___ your children

___ your spouse   ___ a hobby or collection

___ sports     ___ politics

___ church     ___ God

___ a club or organization ___ friends

___ other: _____

Turn and share your rankings with your spouse or a friend. Then as a group, discuss the following:

- **In what ways have your priorities changed since your youth?**

- **What motivates your commitment to the top item on your list?**

**Topics:** Conflict; Peace

**Scripture:** Psalm 34:12-14; Ephesians 4:2-3

From the following list, individually select the situation that would most bother you. After you've made your selection, discuss with your spouse the best way to pursue peace in the situations you've selected. After you've finished, share with the group one of your situations and how you decided to deal with the conflict.

- **You find yourself continually changing the thermostat because your spouse sets it "too hot" or "too cold."**

- **You leave the house late for an appointment and discover that the gas gauge of your car is on empty. (Oh, and your seat is in the wrong position, and all your radio station settings have been changed.)**

- **The phone bill is higher than you think it should be. Someone is using it for more than agreed on.**

- **You've just received a bank statement indicating four $25 charges for overdrawing your checking account.**

- **Guests have been invited for dinner without your knowledge.**

# Trust Busters and Builders

**Topic:** Trust

**Scripture:** Proverbs 3:5-6; Matthew 5:36-37

Form two groups. In one group, brainstorm a list of trust builders—things that can be done to strengthen trust between people. In the other group, brainstorm a list of trust busters—things that tear down the level of trust.

"WHO WOULD YOU TRUST?" PAGE 35

| Trust Builders | Trust Busters |
|----------------|---------------|
|                |               |

After a few minutes, come together to share your lists. Then discuss these questions:

- **What characteristic would you say most distinguishes these lists from each other?**

- **In assessing these lists, which is easier—to build trust or to bust trust? Why?**

# Kingdom Corporation

**Topic:** Stewardship

**Scripture:** Matthew 25:14-30; Luke 19:12-27

Consider yourself an employee of the Kingdom Corporation. The owner, a very powerful and wealthy individual, has to travel for business to a remote area and will be gone for the next two years. You and your associates have been left in charge of managing various company assets.

**Tip:**
For this wrap-up, either assign the various assets or have teams draw for them.

Form three teams. Your team will be assigned one of three assets to manage: (1) one million dollars, (2) the facility (a 100,000-square-foot multiuse facility), or (3) the auto fleet (a dozen brand-new minivans).

Spend five to ten minutes with your team to develop a resource-management plan. Decide how you will manage your assigned resource, and devise a strategy. Then present your plan, including the thinking behind your strategy, to the other teams.

After each team has presented, discuss the following questions:

- **Regardless of your team's asset, what was your team's goal? Why?**

- **Which trait do you think is more important to the owner: action or results? Explain.**

- **How does this activity relate to the way we handle the resources God has given us?**

- **What role does faith play in stewardship?**

# Brian and Linda Revisited

**Topics:** Communication; Listening

**Scripture:** James 1:19

In two groups, look again at the dialogue between Brian and Linda that was presented earlier in this session. In your group, rewrite their exchange based on the components of good listening that you've been discussing. Then each group should present its version of the "new" Brian and Linda. After both groups have made presentations, answer these questions:

"POPCORN,"
PAGE 28

- **What changed in how Brian and Linda communicated in the new scenarios?**

**Supplies:**
To rewrite the original Brian and Linda dialogue, groups will need a copy of the original exchange (pages 28–29).

**For Extra Impact:**
For this wrap-up, consider presenting the rewritten exchange between Brian and Linda in dramatic fashion.

- **How easy is it for you to do the things you know you should do when you communicate with and listen to your spouse? Explain.**

**Topic:** Confrontation

**Scripture:** Ephesians 4:15; Colossians 4:6

In a confrontation, one of the most effective techniques is to turn "you" messages into "I" messages. For example, instead of declaring, "You don't understand me," say, "I feel misunderstood." This helps the person you're talking to focus on the problem rather than on personal failure.

"I" messages are usually clear and honest. "I" messages don't place blame. "You" messages are most often attacks and criticisms. They seek to fix blame on the other person.

A list of "you" messages follows. As a group, take a minute to brainstorm a few more "you" messages to add to the list. Then with your spouse or in a subgroup, turn the "you" messages into "I" messages.

| **"You" Messages** | **"I" Messages** |
| --- | --- |
| You don't understand me! | I feel misunderstood! |
| You don't budget our money! | I'm concerned about our finances. |
| Can you help me? | |
| You are gone too much! | |
| You are always late! | |
| You always blame everything on me! | |
| You make me angry! | |
| You never tell me you love me! | |

Report to the group at large a couple of "I" messages that your subgroup came up with. After each group has reported, take a moment of silence to think about a particular "you" message that you find yourself using often. Pray silently by yourself, asking God to help you communicate better with others.

# Job Descriptions

**Topics:** Husbands; Wives

**Scripture:** John 15:12-13; I Corinthians 13:4-7;
Ephesians 5:21-33

Write a short draft of a job description for you as a husband or wife in the space that follows:

**My Job Description**

"PLEASE PASS THE ROLES," PAGE 19

When you've finished, share with your spouse the job description you've written. After sharing, answer this question together:

- **In what ways can you fulfill your job description during the next week?**

# Stress Builders and Busters

**Topic:** Stress

**Scripture:** Psalm 55:22; Philippians 4:6-7; 1 Peter 5:7

"LIFESTYLES OF THE STRESSED AND FRAZZLED," PAGE 9

As a group, create a "Top Ten" list of stress builders—things in life that create stress.

**Top Ten Stress Builders**

1.

2.

3.

4.

5.

6.

7.

8.

9.

10.

Now brainstorm a list of stress busters in response to the list of stress builders. Then pick a stress buster you want to use this week.

# Be Still

**Topic:** Stillness

**Scripture:** Psalm 37:7; 46:10

Psalm 46:10 encourages us to "Be still, and know that I am God" (NIV). Practice being still before God for five minutes. During this time try to clear your mind of all distractions and focus on God. After the time is up, discuss these questions:

"THE HURRIED FAMILY," PAGE 12

- **How hard was it for you to be still physically? spiritually?**

- **How long did the time seem?**

- **What thoughts went through your mind as you tried to focus on God?**

- **What might be the long-term benefits of regularly taking time to be still before God?**

**Topic:** Work

**Scripture:** Colossians 3:17, 23-24

In thinking about the coming week, what are the top three things you would like to accomplish at work? What are the top three things you would like to accomplish outside of work? List these:

| Work | Life |
|------|------|
| 1. | 1. |
| 2. | 2. |
| 3. | 3. |

After recording your goals, share them with your spouse or a friend. Discuss how you can achieve both lists.

# Marriage Mission Statement

**Topic:** Marriage

**Scripture:** Mark 10:6-9; Hebrews 13:4

Organizations use mission statements to evaluate and plan the direction of their efforts. If you were to have a mission statement for yourself as a husband or wife, what would you like it to say? Individually, answer for yourself the following questions to help you develop a personal mission statement for valuing your husband or wife.

- **Up to this point, what has been your major purpose and direction as a husband or wife?**

- **Looking ahead, what would you like your major purpose and direction as a husband or wife to be?**

- **Draft a one- or two-sentence mission statement for you as a husband or wife.**

After completing the above, share your mission statement with your spouse. Then work together to draft a one- or two-sentence mission statement for your marriage. Keep in mind your statement does not mean that you have already "arrived"; it is simply a statement of what you desire your marriage to become.

**Our Marriage Mission Statement**

After drafting your marriage mission statement, pray as a couple and ask God to help you achieve the purpose he would have for your marriage.

If you're comfortable doing it, share your statement with the group.

# Listen Up! (Epilogue)

**Topics:** Patience; Understanding

**Scripture:** Proverbs 11:12; 14:29; 1 Corinthians 13:4-7

Rod was surprised by Cindy's response. After all, he thought his advice was pretty good. But as he sat in the living room reflecting on what had just transpired, he thought, "I didn't really try to understand Cindy. I just wanted to solve the problems and get on with life."

In separate groups of men and women, revisit the Rod and Cindy case study. In each group discuss what should happen next. After each group has determined what Rod and Cindy should do, present your scenarios (in dramatic fashion if you'd like). Then discuss:

- **What was different about Rod and Cindy's exchange as presented by your groups compared with their first exchange?**

"LISTEN UP!"
PAGE 55

**Supplies:** For this wrap-up, be sure to have a copy of the "Listen Up!" warm-up (pp. 55–56) for reference.

 Hanging Out

**Topic:** Relationships

**Scripture:** Ecclesiastes 4:9-10

As a group, take some time to brainstorm a list of simple, low-cost, relationship-building activities. Consider breaking into subgroups, with each group working on a separate list. For example, depending on the makeup of your group, one group might create a list of activities for parents of young children, while another group might come up with a list of simple, low-cost things to do with friends. Record your ideas in the following space:

**Relationship-Building Activities (for _____ ):**

After compiling your ideas, review them, and select one that you would like to do in the coming week.

**Topics:** Dreams; Failure; Risk

**Scripture:** Matthew 14:22-33

Choose one of the following questions to answer and share with the group:

- **What is one of the riskiest things you have ever done or tried?**

- **What is one thing you dream of trying if you knew you couldn't fail and if money were not an issue?**

- **What failure in your life can you look back on and appreciate in some way?**

- **Read Matthew 14:22-33. Where do you, like Peter, need to exercise faith in your life and "get out of the boat"?**

# Looking Ahead

**Topics:** Future; Planning; Vision

**Scripture:** Proverbs 3:5-6; 14:22; 15:22

The wrap-up for this session provides couples the opportunity and framework to work together to plan for the future in one of five areas: spiritual, relational, professional, financial, and recreational. As a couple, select one of the five areas and work together to draft a plan of what the future might look like for you in the area you've selected. Do this by working through the following steps:

## Step 1

*Vision:* (Where do we want to be in this area in the next few years?)

**Tip:**
If you find this wrap-up beneficial, plan to set aside time with your spouse to work through the steps outlined in this exercise as a planning tool for all five of the areas mentioned.

- **One year:**

- **Three years:**

## Step 2

*Goals:* (What do we want to accomplish in the next few years?)

- **One year:**

- **Three years:**

## Step 3

*Resources:* (What do we need [for example, people or funds] to achieve our vision and goals?)

## Step 4

*Action Steps:* (What incremental steps do we need to take to accomplish our vision and goals? What is the first step we should take?)

Time permitting, couples should each select one aspect of the plan they've discussed—the couple's vision, a goal, a resource, or an action step—to report to the group.

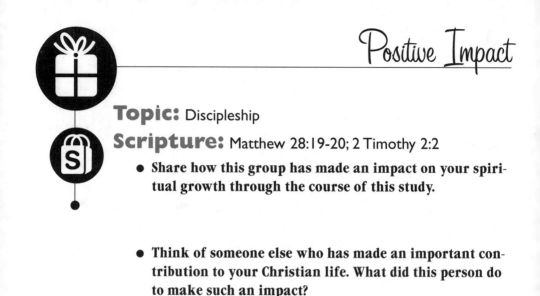

**Topic:** Discipleship

**Scripture:** Matthew 28:19-20; 2 Timothy 2:2

- Share how this group has made an impact on your spiritual growth through the course of this study.

- Think of someone else who has made an important contribution to your Christian life. What did this person do to make such an impact?

**Supplies:** For this wrap-up, everyone will need a blank sheet of paper and a pen or pencil.

- How did this person "replicate" himself or herself in you?

Using a pen or pencil, trace around your hand on paper. Then discuss these questions:

- How does drawing your hand illustrate duplicating yourself as you seek to make disciples for Jesus?

- What things might you *not* want to see duplicated in someone else?

- Now on each finger of your drawing, write something you feel you should change in your life to become a better disciple maker. Take home your paper, and post it where it will remind you of what you want to improve in your relationship with God and others.

# High Hopes

**Topic:** Hope

**Scripture:** Proverbs 23:18; Isaiah 40:31; Romans 15:4

Choose one or two of the following questions to answer and share with the group:

- **What do you remember hoping for when you were a child?**

- **What hope do you have for either yourself, your marriage, your spouse, or your children?**

- **What is one thing that gives you hope for the future?**

- **When was hope restored in your life?**

# What Would You Do?

**Topic:** Confrontation

**Scripture:** Galatians 5:1-2

As a couple, pick two of the following scenarios, and discuss with your spouse what you most likely would do in each situation.

- You are at the store and notice someone shoplifting.

- You observe a co-worker repeatedly take home office supplies.

- Your in-laws keep dropping by unexpectedly.

- You find out at a parent-teacher conference that your child has not been turning in homework assignments.

- Your spouse promised to be home at a certain time, but arrives thirty minutes late.

After discussing with your spouse the scenarios you've picked, tell the group about your responses.

After everyone has had a chance to share, answer this question:

- **How is confrontation in marriage different from confrontation with a stranger, family, or co-worker?**

# Character Traits

**Topic:** Character

**Scripture:** Romans 5:3-4; Galatians 5:22-23

From the following list of personal characteristics, circle the three you think are most important.

| | | |
|---|---|---|
| trustworthy | humble | teachable |
| obedient | kind | persevering |
| respectful | self-controlled | hopeful |
| loving | cooperative | faithful |
| honest | joyful | friendly |
| courageous | patient | forgiving |
| generous | fair | gentle |

After everyone has made a selection, discuss what characteristics you chose and why.

**Bonus question:** Depending on the makeup of your group, you also may want to include the following as part of this wrap-up: **What two or three words from the list do you believe are characteristic of your spouse? With your spouse, share the words you've selected and why.**

# Watch Your Mouth

**Topic:** Confrontation

**Scripture:** Proverbs 15:1; Ephesians 4:29

Pick a couple of the following scenarios, and discuss with your spouse how you would most likely respond. Remember, be kind—and have fun with this!

- You receive a notice that your auto insurance rates are going up because of a recent speeding ticket. Your spouse has neglected to tell you about getting the ticket.

- You are lost, but your spouse refuses to stop and ask for directions.

- You notice that your spouse is using your favorite T-shirt to clean the bathroom.

- Your spouse was going to stop at the cleaners to pick up the outfit you plan to wear tomorrow to an important meeting. Your spouse arrives home having forgotten to go by the cleaners, and now the cleaners is closed.

Now go back through the scenarios you've discussed, and in place of what your likely response would be, talk about what "loving confrontation" might look like in each situation. Then report to the group about one of the scenarios.

# Bouncing Balloons

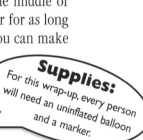

**Topic:** Application

**Scripture:** Romans 7:14-23; 8:9-15

Pass around balloons and markers. Blow up and tie your balloon, and then write on your balloon as many of the practical things you've learned about during the course of this lesson or study. When everyone's balloon is ready, toss the balloons into the air in the middle of the group. As a group, try to keep all the balloons in the air for as long as you can. You may want to keep time to see how long you can make it. Try this a couple times to see whether you can improve on your time. When you've finished, pick up the balloon closest to you, and answer these questions:

**Supplies:** For this wrap-up, every person will need an uninflated balloon and a marker.

- **What does the balloon you are holding say?**

- **How easy was it to keep up all the balloons?**

- **How easy do you find it to do everything you know that you should?**

**Topic:** Service

**Scripture:** Matthew 25:31-40

As a demonstration of following God, plan a community service project with your group. You might work with a homeless shelter, a food bank, a home-repair agency, or a church ministry. Begin planning this week, solidify your plans by next week, and try to do the project within a week or two after that. Be sure to talk afterward about the experience, and consider additional projects that God might want you involved in.

**Our group service project (notes):**

# Steps Toward Transparency

**Topic:** Transparency

**Scripture:** Colossians 3:12-14

Step 1. *Be open with God.*

Step 2. *Create an atmosphere of love, commitment, and forgiveness in your home.*

Step 3. *Affirm your spouse when he or she practices transparency.*

Step 4. *Pray regularly with each other.*

- As a group, review Step 1 by discussing some practical ways that you can be open with God. What have you found to be helpful?

- To review Steps 2 and 3, turn to your spouse and discuss ways you can create an atmosphere that promotes greater transparency between you; then talk about ways you can affirm each other, or talk about a time when your spouse was transparent with you that you really appreciated.

- Practice Step 4 by making plans to pray together at least three times this week. Pray now for each other that God would help you to be transparent with him and with your spouse.

*Field Trip*

**Topic:** Giving

**Scripture:** Proverbs 19:17; Luke 6:38; Acts 20:35; James 1:27

This is a fun, hands-on experience that can help you determine where to give (above and beyond the financial support of your local church).

As a group, visit a local Christian ministry or nonprofit community service provider that you may have an interest in supporting and determine

- its financial needs.

- how well it uses financial resources.

- its ministry results.

- its ministry objectives.

If visiting a ministry is not feasible, consider writing to a ministry or visiting its Web site to determine the above.

# Steps

**Topic:** Respect

**Scripture:** Ephesians 5:33; I Peter 3:7

Spread out as much as possible in your meeting area, but stay with your spouse. Stand facing your spouse. Then listen as the leader reads the following descriptive statements. After each statement is read, take one step back (regardless of whether you have done what the statement describes).

- You have arrived home later than you said you would.
- You have committed your spouse and yourself to plans without first checking with your "better half."
- You have made a comment critical of your spouse's mother.
- You have been impatient with your spouse.
- You forgot your anniversary or your spouse's birthday.

Now take one step toward your spouse after the leader reads each of these statements:

- You regularly pray together as a couple.
- You often compliment your spouse.
- You take time to talk about each other's day.
- You go out together, just the two of you, for no particular reason.
- You say nice things about your spouse's family.
- You apologize when you make a mistake.

Discuss the following questions:

- **How did you feel during the first half of the experience? the second half?**

- **How is this experience like what happens in marriage?**

# Taking Out the Trash

**Topic:** Chores

**Scripture:** Philippians 2:14-16; Colossians 3:23-24

Take a minute to reminisce about the chores you had to do when you were a kid.

- **Which of these was your least favorite? Why?**

- **How are the chores you do now different from the chores you did in your youth?**

- **Of the tasks you currently do, which is your most and least favorite?**

- **What task or chore does someone do for you on a regular basis for which you are particularly grateful?**

# A to Z

**Topics:** Affirmation; Words

**Scripture:** Proverbs 16:24; 25:11

To close this session, see whether you can compliment one another all the way through the alphabet! For example, start with the letter A, and take turns saying something affirming to someone else in the group, such as, "I *appreciate* you." Then go on to the letter B, trying to make it all the way through the alphabet. If you make it through once, you may want to try for a second time.

A:                          N:

B:                          O:

C:                          P:

D:                          Q:

E:                          R:

F:                          S:

G:                          T:

H:                          U:

I:                          V:

J:                          W:

K:                          X:

L:                          Y:

M:                          Z:

# Our Perfect Day

**Topic:** Time together

**Scripture:** Psalm 118:24; Romans 14:5-8

An important part of commitment in marriage is making a priority of spending time together. Close this session by spending some time to plan the "perfect day" for yourselves as a couple:

- On our perfect day, we would get up at...

- For breakfast, we would...

- We would spend most of the day...

- Something special we would do is...

- And finally, we would end our "perfect day" together by...

Share one thing with the group about the day you've planned.

# Recap

**Topic:** Assessment

**Scripture:** I Thessalonians 5:15, 21

## Round 1

On a slip of paper, write a one- or two-word response to complete the following sentence:

- **How I felt about coming to this group tonight was**

_____ .

When everyone has finished, pass the slips of paper to the leader. (Note: Do not sign your paper; your response should be anonymous.) The leader then will complete the sentence by sharing from the slips of paper.

**Supplies:** For this wrap-up, everyone will need a couple of index cards or slips of paper and a pen or pencil.

## Round 2

On a slip of paper, write a one- or two-word response to complete the following sentence:

- **How I feel now, after going through this session, is**

_____ .

When everyone has finished, pass the slips of paper to the leader. The leader then will complete the sentence by sharing from the slips of paper.

**Tip:** This wrap-up is recommended for the first session of a course or study.

## Round 3

As a group, discuss some ways this group can encourage and support its members during the course of this study.

# Fresh Start

**Topics:** Budget; Financial priorities

**Scripture:** I Timothy 5:8

Imagine that your financial slate has been wiped clean. You have no debt or current financial obligations, and your income is equal to your current earnings. In other words, you're starting over. Assign the percentage of net income you would allocate to each of the following categories (a description of these categories is on the next page).

| | |
|---|---|
| charitable giving | _____ % |
| savings | _____ |
| housing | _____ |
| food | _____ |
| clothing | _____ |
| transportation | _____ |
| entertainment | _____ |
| medical | _____ |
| insurance | _____ |
| children | _____ |
| gifts | _____ |
| miscellaneous | _____ |
| **Total:** | **100%** |

After assigning your percentages, discuss these questions:

- **Which allocation would change most if you were given a fresh start? Which would change least?**


- **What would be the best thing about a fresh start?**

**Charitable giving:** tithe, missionary support, and other charitable causes

**Savings:** contributions to 401Ks and IRAs and deposits to a savings account and other investments.

**Housing:** mortgage, rent, homeowners or renters insurance, property taxes, utilities (gas, electric, phone, trash, sewer, and water), cleaning, repairs, and maintenance

**Food:** groceries (Do not include the cost of dining out.)

**Clothing:** accessories and family members' wardrobes

**Transportation:** car payment, auto insurance, gas, oil, parking, repairs, and maintenance

**Entertainment:** dining out, movies, concerts, plays, sporting events, baby sitters, magazines, newspapers, vacations, club dues, and recreational activities

**Medical:** medical, dental, and vision insurance; doctor and dentist payments; and medication

**Insurance:** life insurance, disability insurance, and any other insurance (except home, auto, or medical)

**Children:** school lunches and supplies, lessons (such as music and dance), tuition, allowance, and child care

**Gifts:** Christmas, birthday, wedding, anniversary, and graduation presents

**Miscellaneous:** dry cleaning, laundry, animal care, hair care, toiletries, and anything not covered in the previous categories

# Hi Honey, I'm Home

**Topic:** Marriage

**Scripture:** Ephesians 5:21-33

Any discussion about biblical responsibilities in marriage can lead to sharp disagreements. Many people bring to the debate their own views shaped by experience, their childhoods, and how their philosophies have been shaped by the world we live in. With your spouse, select one of the following statements to discuss. From what you've studied about how God views marriage, talk about how you would respond. After each couple has had time to talk about the statement it selected, share your responses with the group.

**Ward:** I think all marriages should be the way it was when I was growing up—you know, "traditional." The man should bring home the bacon, and the woman should fry it up in the pan.

**Gloria:** Essentially, the institution of marriage exists to oppress women. I mean, a woman gets married and is supposed to change her name? It's like you're not your own person anymore. A woman is equal to a man and shouldn't lower herself to the subjection of marriage.

**Gilbert:** Marriage should be an equal partnership. The only specific responsibilities a husband or wife should assume are ones that have been mutually agreed upon, based on each other's gifts and abilities.

# I Owe You

**Topic:** Gratitude

**Scripture:** Romans 13:8

Take a minute to consider some nonfinancial debts you owe.

- **To whom do you owe a "debt" of gratitude or a debt of love? Think of someone, and tell the group who you are thinking about and what nonfinancial debt you owe that person.**

- **What could you do to "pay" this person? Discuss some ideas such as sending a card or e-mail, making a phone call or baking some cookies, and plan to follow through with a "payment" this week.**

# A Few of Your Favorite Things

**Topic:** Favorites

**Scripture:** Proverbs 18:15

How well do you really know your spouse? Take the following quiz and find out!

## Complete the following sentences:

My spouse's favorite color is...

My spouse's favorite TV show is...

My spouse's favorite movie is...

My spouse's favorite book is...

My spouse's favorite flavor of ice cream is...

My spouse's favorite store is...

My spouse's favorite room in the house is...

My spouse's favorite time of the day is...

My spouse's favorite season of the year is...

My spouse's favorite vacation spot is...

My spouse's favorite radio station is...

After you answer these questions, get with your spouse to see how you did. Then as a group, discuss this question:

- **What practical things can we do to know our spouses better?**

# 168-Hour Week (Part 2)

**Topics:** Priorities; Time

**Scripture:** Ecclesiastes 3:1-8; Ephesians 5:15-17

We all have 168 hours to spend each week. Think about how you would like to spend your time—not how you do spend it, but how you would like to spend a typical week. Fill out the following time sheet accordingly:

"168-HOUR WEEK," PAGE 22

__ work (your primary job—include getting ready and commuting time)

__ sleep (include getting ready for bed)

__ exercise

__ other work (things like household chores)

__ TV or computer (personal Web surfing, e-mail)

__ marriage (time spent with your spouse)

__ family/friends (time spent with kids, extended family, and friends)

__ God (include Bible study, prayer, and time at church)

__ errands/shopping

__ meals (include preparation time)

__ other: _____

**Total: 168 hours**

After you have completed your time sheets, discuss the following:

- **What are one or two things that you would most like to change in your current schedule to move closer to your desired schedule?**

# How's the Weather?

**Topic:** Family relationships

**Scripture:** Ephesians 4:1-3; Colossians 3:12-14

Think about your relationships with the members of your family, concentrating first on the members of your immediate family but also including your extended family as time permits. Describe to the group in terms of the weather how you feel about one relationship. For example, you might say, "About our oldest son, I'm feeling like it's partly cloudy with a chance of rain." Take turns sharing weather reports.

**Tip:**
This wrap-up is best for a group that has been meeting together regularly.

After everyone who wants to has had a chance to give a report, pray as a group about the relationships you've discussed.

# Bearing One Another's Burdens

**Topics:** Advice; Prayer

**Scripture:** Proverbs 19:20; Matthew 18:19-20;
Acts 2:42; James 5:16

Answer the following two questions individually:

- **If you could ask the group for advice on just one thing, what would it be? Write this question on an index card or piece of paper.**

- **What is one issue or concern in your life that you are dealing with right now? If you were to state this as a prayer request, what would it be? Write your request on an index card or piece of paper.**

**Supplies:**
For this wrap-up, everyone will need index cards or paper and a pen or pencil.

Now, if comfortable doing so, turn in your question and request to the leader.

As part of the wrap-up and the regular closing prayer time for this and any remaining sessions, your leader will randomly select one or two cards to read to the group. For questions, the group members will take a few minutes to offer any advice they have on those subjects. If you have experience with an issue someone has raised, you may relate to the group what was helpful to you in that situation.

**Tip:**
This exercise is best used with a group that has been together for a while.

For prayer requests, the group will spend a few moments praying for the situation.

## Topics: Forgiveness; Reconciliation

## Scripture: Mark 11:25; 2 Corinthians 5:18-19

Everyone in the group should take hold of an object; a book will do, but the bigger and bulkier the item, the better. Firmly hold your object with both hands, and don't let go. Now turn to another person and attempt to shake hands. After attempting this, discuss this question:

- **What problems did you encounter in trying to connect with your partner?**

**Supplies:** For this wrap-up, everyone will need one thing to hold onto. A Bible, book, or notebook would do, but the bigger and bulkier, the better.

Now try it again, this time without the objects.

- **What was different this time?**

- **In what way is this exercise like extending forgiveness or being reconciled to another?**

# Moving Forward

**Topic:** Spiritual disciplines

**Scripture:** Isaiah 55:6; Luke 11:9-10; Hebrews 10:19-23

Spread out as much as possible in your meeting area, but stay with your spouse. Stand side by side with your spouse, facing the same direction, and move apart about three feet. Place one of your books on the floor several steps out in front of you. Then listen as your leader reads the following descriptive statements. After each statement, take one small step toward your book. It doesn't matter whether you do what the statement describes, take a step after each one.

- You maintain a regular personal quiet time and share insights with your spouse.

- You share together how that week's sermon affected you.

- You pray together.

- You have devotions together.

- You apply the Bible's principles to your personal life and marriage.

- You seek God's will in your decisions.

Discuss the following questions in your group:

- **What happened to the distance between you and your spouse as you moved toward your book?**

- **How is this like what happens when you seek to draw closer to God in your lives and marriages?**

- **How would doing what the statements said make a difference in communication within your marriage?**

# Topical Index

# Checklist

| Warm-Ups | Dates Used | Group or Class Used With | Notes/ Comments |
|---|---|---|---|
| Lifestyles of the Stressed and Frazzled | | | |
| The Day We Wed | | | |
| Leader or Servant? | | | |
| The Hurried Family | | | |
| Getting to Know You | | | |
| A Team Sport | | | |
| Likely Responses | | | |
| A Match Made in Paradise | | | |
| Please Pass the Roles | | | |
| Best Friends | | | |
| Dream House | | | |
| 168-Hour Week | | | |
| Down Memory Lane | | | |
| Guess Who | | | |
| A Piece of the Pie | | | |
| Practiced Prayer | | | |
| I Love to Tell the Story | | | |
| Popcorn | | | |
| Invisible Power | | | |
| Reflections | | | |
| Minor Irritations | | | |
| Commitments | | | |
| Typical Trials | | | |
| Who Would You Trust? | | | |
| By the Numbers | | | |
| May I Borrow Your Car? | | | |

| | Dates Used | Group or Class Used With | Notes/ Comments |
|---|---|---|---|
| Thank You, Aunt Harriet! | | | |
| Bad Hair Day? | | | |
| The Way We Were | | | |
| What I Like, How About You? | | | |
| As Advertised | | | |
| Vive la Différence! | | | |
| Giving It Away | | | |
| Something Between Us | | | |
| To Err Is Human, to Forgive Divine | | | |
| Insults and Blessings | | | |
| Interview | | | |
| My Cup Runneth Over | | | |
| Loose Change | | | |
| Strings Attached | | | |
| Hard Times | | | |
| Your Spiritual Heritage | | | |
| Follow the Leader | | | |
| Listen Up! | | | |
| Won't You Be My Neighbor? | | | |
| Who Are You? | | | |
| How Was Your Day? | | | |
| Daydreams | | | |
| Neither a Borrower nor Lender Be? | | | |
| House of Cards | | | |
| That Makes Me Mad! | | | |
| The In-Laws | | | |

| Wrap-Ups | Dates Used | Group or Class Used With | Notes/ Comments |
|---|---|---|---|
| Where Do We Go From Here? | | | |
| Thanks for Your Support! | | | |
| A Look at Love | | | |
| Another Piece of the Pie | | | |
| It's Puzzling | | | |
| Serving Each Other | | | |
| Positive Attributes | | | |
| Paper-Thin Skin | | | |
| Following God | | | |
| Wishing-Not Well | | | |
| Recipe for Relationships | | | |
| Committed | | | |
| Bothersome Behaviors | | | |
| Trust Busters and Builders | | | |
| Kingdom Corporation | | | |
| Brian and Linda Revisited | | | |
| You and I | | | |
| Job Descriptions | | | |
| Stress Builders and Busters | | | |
| Be Still | | | |
| To Do List | | | |
| Marriage Mission Statement | | | |
| Listen Up! (Epilogue) | | | |
| Hanging Out | | | |
| Big Dreams | | | |
| Looking Ahead | | | |

| | Dates Used | Group or Class Used With | Notes/ Comments |
|---|---|---|---|
| Positive Impact | | | |
| High Hopes | | | |
| What Would You Do? | | | |
| Character Traits | | | |
| Watch Your Mouth | | | |
| Bouncing Balloons | | | |
| Community Service | | | |
| Steps Toward Transparency | | | |
| Field Trip | | | |
| Steps | | | |
| Taking Out the Trash | | | |
| A to Z | | | |
| Our Perfect Day | | | |
| Recap | | | |
| Fresh Start | | | |
| Hi Honey, I'm Home | | | |
| I Owe You | | | |
| A Few of Your Favorite Things | | | |
| 168-Hour Week (Part 2) | | | |
| How's the Weather? | | | |
| Bearing One Another's Burdens | | | |
| Letting Go | | | |
| Moving Forward | | | |

CHECKLIST

Group Publishing, Inc.
Attention: Product Development
P.O. Box 481
Loveland, CO 80539
Fax: (970) 679-4370

# Evaluation for
## *Warm-Ups and Wrap-Ups*

Please help Group Publishing, Inc., continue to provide innovative and useful resources for ministry. Please take a moment to fill out this evaluation and mail or fax it to us. Thanks!

● ● ●

1. As a whole, this book has been (circle one)

not very helpful                                                                 very helpful

1        2        3        4        5        6        7        8        9        10

2. The best things about this book:


3. Ways this book could be improved:


4. Things I will change because of this book:


5. Other books I'd like to see Group publish in the future:


6. Would you be interested in field-testing future Group products and giving us your feedback? If so, please fill in the information below:

Name_____

Church Name _____

Denomination _____ Church Size _____

Church Address _____

City _____ State _____ ZIP _____

Church Phone _____

E-mail _____

# Discover the secrets to lifelong marriage.